Contents

How it all started

A kind of football

No one really knows how football started, but it has been around for a very long time. The Romans came to Britain more than 2,000 years ago and they used to play a kind of football game.

In the Middle Ages, whole villages joined in games of football. But they weren't like the football we see today. The game took place across fields and over rivers.

A rubber latex bladder forms the basis of footballs today.

Football in the Middle Ages was a very rough and risky game.

Anywhere the ball went the game went after it. And anyone could join in. Most of the time they used a pig's bladder as a ball, but anything would do.

They didn't have any proper rules so things could get nasty. Lots of people were killed playing football in those days. About 700 years ago, the King tried to ban football. He said it was too noisy and dangerous. Anyone caught playing football could be thrown in prison.

The Football Association

When football started the laws were very simple. There were no goal posts. The pitch could be any size. You could kick the ball, throw it, or pick it up and carry it. The first team to score was the winner. So a game might be over very quickly, or it might take all day.

Then they began to make up laws. One of the first laws was about passing. You were not allowed to pass the ball forward. They still have this law in rugby today.

Passing backwards during a rugby game

The original Football Association logo

About 200 years ago, people formed the first football clubs. Each club made up its own laws, so there were lots of muddles and arguments.

The clubs got together to stop this. They made up laws for everyone. They called themselves the FA – the Football Association.

It's in the laws

Today there are lots of laws. How well do you know them? Can you say whether these laws are true or false?

1 You can only be sent off when play begins.

2 You can score a goal directly from a corner.

3 The goalie can always handle the ball in the penalty area.

4 You can't be off-side from a throw-in.

5 The goalie isn't allowed to move when a penalty is being taken.

Referee's cards
and whistle.

5 False: he can move from side to side, but he can't come forwards.

4 True: you can't be off-side from a goal-kick either.

3 False: the goalie can't handle the ball from a back-pass.

2 True: these days you can score from a goal-kick as well.

1 False: you can be sent off even before the game starts.

Fam⚽us clubs

North and South

The first professional football league started in the North and the Midlands. It was called the Football Association (FA).

The teams from the South were not professional, so they could not join. The first one that did join was Woolwich Arsenal. In 1871 the FA ran a knock-out cup for the clubs. This was the FA Cup, and it's still going today.

Arsenal are nicknamed The Gunners because they used to be based in Woolwich near the Royal Armoury.

The league championship began later, in 1888. The oldest of all the league clubs is Notts County. But, Preston North End was the most successful team in those early days. They scored the first ever league goal and won the first ever league championship.

Preston North End in league championship action.

The double

For 64 years, no one managed to win the league and the cup in the same year. This is called doing 'the double'. In 1961, the London team Tottenham Hotspur (Spurs) did 'the double' for the first time in the twentieth century.

Spurs playing well in 1961.

Real Madrid have won the European Cup eight times.

In 1955 there was a new competition for all the best clubs in Europe – the European Cup. For the first five years the European Cup was won by a team from Spain – Real Madrid. The first British team to win the European Cup was Celtic in 1967.

The Busby Babes

Today, Manchester United is one of the biggest clubs in the world. Fifty years ago they had a team of brilliant players. The manager was Sir Matt Busby. The team was called The Busby Babes because most of the players were so young.

In 1958 The Busby Babes flew to Germany to play a game. There was a terrible plane crash and eight of that famous team were killed.

The Busby Babes in 1958

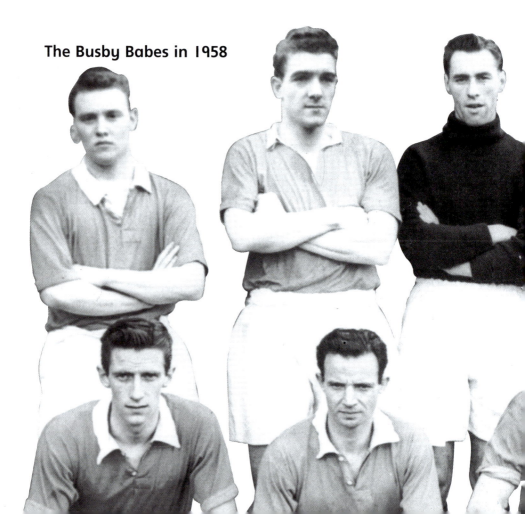

Sir Matt Busby talking to his team just before they won the European Cup.

Sir Matt Busby was badly injured but he lived to build up a new team. Ten years later, his new Manchester United became the first English club to win the European Cup.

The treble

In 1999, with Sir Alex Ferguson as their manager, Manchester United did 'the treble'. They won the league, the FA Cup and the European Cup.

Ole Gunnar Solksjaer shoots for goal.

Manchester United holding up the European Cup
in triumph.

The World Cup

The early days

Football's biggest competition is for the Jules Rimet trophy. We call it the World Cup.

These days, lots of countries try to win a place in the finals, but when the World Cup first started only 13 countries took part. That was in 1930, in Uruguay, South America. None of the British teams was there.

The 1930 World Cup programme

The great hunt ends in a suburban garden

Daily Mirror

Monday, March 28, 1966   No. 19,365

MAN AND A DOG FIND THE WORLD CUP

The Mirror's Verdict:

WILSON CAN DO IT!

But, this time, no alibis

THERE is no need for the politicians, the Press or the TV commentators to be restless or puzzled any longer. The Daily Mirror is doing precisely what it said it would do: **FIRST THE INQUEST ON THE TWO PRINCIPAL PARTIES—THEN, IN THE LAST WEEK OF THE ELECTION, THE VERDICT.**

Here's the verdict, bang on time.

❶ The Mirror believes that the country has no alternative but to send Mr. Wilson back to Downing-street and his Labour Government back to power.

❷ The Mirror hopes that Mr. Wilson's majority will be large enough to enable him to carry on the good works that have already reached blueprint or legislation stage and to tackle with new resolve and no alibis the two major hurdles which threw their Tory predecessors—horses, jockeys, trainers and all.

❸ The Mirror pleads for immediate action on the balance of payments and productivity problem —still desperately urgent but still involved—and for early decisions

Mirror Comment

By MIRROR REPORTER

THE World Cup was found in the garden of a house in South London.

A man taking his dog for a walk saw something glinting. He picked it up. It was the missing world-gold Soccer trophy.

The man took it at once to Gipsy Hill police station, West Norwood, and handed it over the counter.

Police took it to Cannon-row police station in West End after duty for fingerprints.

The garden where the trophy was found belongs to a large four-storey Victorian house in Beulah-hill, a main road used by thousands every day.

The house is divided into flats, and the man who found the trophy lives in the basement flat.

Value

Police believe that the £30,000 high insured for £30,000 but with a basic value of about £2,000 was abandoned in a panic by someone who believed that Scotland Yard's Flying Squad was on his trail.

They think the cup was tossed over the 10ft. high hedge running in front of the garden.

Police at Gipsy Hill said the cup appeared to be undamaged.

The lid was sent last Wednesday in a brown paper parcel to Football Association chairman Joe Mears.

Saved

Mr. Mears said last night: "I'm very pleased the cup has been found.

"This has saved our honour in the eyes of the world."

Anjanette joins

In 1966 the famous World Cup trophy went missing. People were afraid there would be no cup for the final. Then, it was found in someone's garden – by a little dog called Pickles!

The famous World Cup trophy

England's victory

England won the trophy in 1966. They beat West Germany 4–2 after extra time. All England's goals were scored by players from West Ham.

Martin Peters scored one and Geoff Hurst scored a hat-trick – the only hat-trick in a World Cup final. The England captain, Bobby Moore, was also from West Ham.

Geoff Hurst playing on top form during his hat-trick season.

The England team victoriously holding the World Cup

Hat-trick
This is when someone scores three goals in a match. Geoff Hurst scored three goals in a match.

FACT

When Brazil won in 1994, it was their fourth time as champions of the world. Italy and West Germany have each won three times.

084

C

Football's finest

Matthews, Lineker or Charlton?

Who was England's greatest player?

A lot of people think it was Stanley Matthews. He came from Stoke, and he played for England until he was 42. Stanley Matthews carried on playing professional football until he was 50. In all that time he was never booked.

Stanley Matthews playing in the 1953 FA Cup Final.

Gary Lineker played for Tottenham Hotspur from 1989 to 1992.

FACT

Gary Lineker was another player who was never booked. He scored 48 goals for England. Only Bobby Charlton with 49 has scored more.

Banks v Pele

England's greatest goalkeeper was Gordon Banks. He was in goal when England won the World Cup in 1966.

Four years later, he was in goal again when England played Brazil. The best footballer in the world – Pele – thought he had scored from a close-range header. But Banks made one of the most brilliant saves ever seen.

FACT

Banks used his goal-saving skills to catch a dog that wandered onto the pitch during a game!

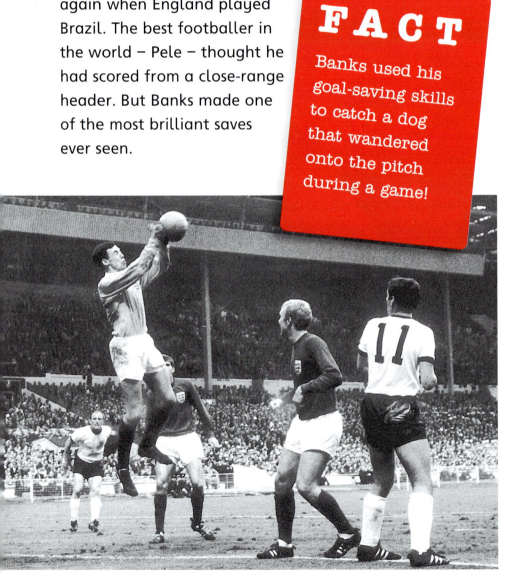

Banks saves the day again.

A dramatic shot by Pele.

FACT

Pele was only 17 when he won his first World Cup medal for Brazil. He scored over a thousand goals in his professional career.

5   084

C

Index

If you have enjoyed reading about football, why not visit www.footee.net, a website that combines fun, football and education.